**Books are to be returned on or before
the last date below.**

LIBREX —

A Portrait in Verse of Royal Tunbridge Wells

WELLSPRING

✺

Colin Aston

with illustrations by Angela Barnes

Colin Aston

Heartland 🙢 **Publishing**

First published in 1995 by Heartland Publishing
55 Cherryfields, Sittingbourne, Kent ME10 1YW

ISBN 0 9525187 1 6

British Library Cataloguing-in-Publication Data
A catalogue record for this book is available
from the British Library.

Typeset in Adobe Caslon by the publisher.

Printed and bound in Great Britain by
Whitstable Litho Printers Ltd., Whitstable, Kent.

*This collection is
dedicated to Anne,
in love and friendship.*

Errata: p. 11 Line 4 : 'always' should be italicised

p. 13 Line 4 : this is first draft inserted by mistake.
should read :
"We can eclipse them with a wink."

CA

Two poems included by publisher's request.
Guess which!

Acknowledgements

Thanks are due to my family and those who have freely offered their thoughts and memories of Royal Tunbridge Wells. Ray Styles has many anecdotes, having lived in the town for sixty years. Pat, Chris and Tim are among the many friends who have offered practical suggestions, and Nick and Jeff's enthusiasm has been invaluable. Where possible I have drawn on these sources to develop new poems, and the responsibility for interpretation is mine.

Thanks are also due to the staff of Tunbridge Wells Library for their helpfulness. I have been indebted in particular to Alan Savidge's book *Royal Tunbridge Wells* (Midas Press, 1975) for factual reference, and would recommend the bibliography within to those interested in the Royal Borough. The two collections entitled *Tunbridge Wells In Old Photographs* compiled by Michael Rowlands and Ian Beavis (Alan Sutton Publishing, 1991 and 1994) are fascinating.

I appreciate the permission to use trade names and slogans where it has been granted, and have no connection with the firms concerned other than as a satisfied customer. The courses of action suggested in *I'm Not A Burglar, I'm A Poet* and *How To Get There* are **not** recommended, and the attitudes of characters portrayed throughout are imaginary. Similarity to any living person is entirely coincidental.

Author's Note

All the locations mentioned in this book are either open to the public or visible from a public footpath. Please respect the privacy of the residents of Royal Tunbridge Wells.

Colin Aston

Tunbridge Wells
April 1995

Contents

Wellspring

Me, I like springs. Wells remind me of fonts
Carved like churchwardens from good Kentish stone
Those good strong basses who hold the sopranos
With their always boom of deep cool water

Springs more than brooks. Brooks are in passing
Friends of the moon, switchblades in lanes
Stormchasing vagabonds, crystal-ball travellers
Gone with tomorrow, what did you expect?

Springs I could live by. Splashed water baptises
Dabchicks and minnows in watercress beds
To names we don't know about, freshens their living
Unquenchably certain desire for love.

They're here all around us. Close by the Wells
Course crookedy brooks jostling down from the Common
And silver springs rising. They swirl in communion
The welcoming sound of many waters.

The Way Around

The Way Around

The guided walks are quite succinct
The long and short of Tunbridge Wells
A mile or two of steady viewing
Passing such time as we can spare

A pleasant start along the Pantiles
Tucks us into history
Sedans, antiques, the long-established
Strolling-through society

King Charles's chapel is a cool reminder:
Contributions from the dutiful
Draw local nature into glory:
Doing good by making beautiful

The stucco mansions of Mount Sion
Gather ivies, gather balconies
Like the fluttering, rustling petticoats
Of lauded ladies sweeping by

Children spangle across the Grove
As the bursting of irregular narcissi
Trumpets freedom to the tall
Uprights of maturity

Close to the bandstand in Calverly Park
We can take coffee, relax in white chairs
While the scents of rose and comfortable lavender
Wash our world in watercolour.

Leaving the park, there's an elegant view
Under the arch of Victoria Lodge
Of the hedge of the Crescent, the passing of ages
The edge of the present, the frame of the new

The Town Hall has its functional
Panes of glass exactly regular
White-rimmed and functional
Panes of glass exactly regular

Museums are always worth a visit
With their catalogues and geologic chunks
Their stuffed birds and their sweet dolls' houses
Postcards of our souvenirs

Sunshine licks at the mintiest domes
An architecture of pleasure and welcome
Rolls the swell of a flouncy facade
You can hear applause if you pick up the shell

Escalators in the Royal Vic
Launch their circulating streams
With the silvery flash of salmon rising
From their rapid shift cascading

How many roads is the song of the busker
One road returning and one where we've wandered
One to the roundabout, one through high offices
One past the lodgings. Hey, Bobby, it's five.

Villas spring from the rock like yachts in rough weather
Buffeting out of the parting of grass
With a filled wake behind them, their pillars of pine
Chuffs of chucked sailcloth on following masts

These high seats have another perspective
Some gin-and-tonic on a tray
A panorama of the town
The attractive prospect of freewheeling down

Trust is this avenue like a cathedral
Arches and aisles of immaculate stain
With a rood-screen of sapphire, it's where to be wedded
To live and give life, assent and descend

Haloed by benches and brilliant sky
The pavilion spills the best side of summer
Some running, some ambling, some flexing old muscles
Spring-heeled as the breeze when the umpire calls play

Where Major York meets Fir Tree Road
The gorse and bracken nearly hide
A pool of quiet for the deaf
A glade made for a photograph

A path shows all seasons, twigs brittle as frost,
Moss sodden as rain, rock hardened as sun
Shambles of falling, footprints reflecting
Angles of woodland, tangles of bramble

Stop-starting squirrels, spun reels on a jackpot
Pinballing ants running up random scores
Cardsharping magpies, fixing their packs
This place is so busy, it's like an arcade

The sculpture of fungus on a long-fallen branch
Attracts a critical blackbird which cocks its young head
This way and that, considering all options
Then chants its refrain of *do I detect...*

Under cool canopies, nothing can reach us
Pattering creatures can never be seen
If we keep raising shadow we'll always be comfy
The oaks of the Common console Castle Road

By the zebra crossing there's a little well
What on earth it's doing there, perhaps the plaque will tell
It may be quite original but now it's hardly scenic
You can stand in front of it to make it photogenic

From the trafficking of Eridge Road
It's a set of steps back to the past
Strolling through white colonnades
To the Bath House and the ironic spring

We've done the tour. This roll of film
Is all used up. Let's take it in
Make some enlargements, pass them on
To entertain our next-of-kin.

Front Gardens

Preludes

Overtures
Miniatures on ivory

Glissandos of green nasturtium
Waterfall luxuriously across the brink

Wind-dried heads of spent hydrangea:
High G's smothered in wintery moths

Threaded webs vibrating to the touch
A clef for rising daffodils

White rocks counterpointing bark:
Plain dotted with botany

An overflow of variegation:
Ivy plays its cadenza in two tones

Green-fingered exercises
Sight sonatas

Miniatures on ivory

Dowding

Between Mount Pleasant's rich displays
And the municipal vision of the Great Hall
Is a memorial swathed in unfamiliar lichen
Beyond, gentle mounds of summer grass

Only a cone of ruddy stone
Plonked down like a spare part
Only the tailplane showing
Of an exceptional airman fallen to ground

My grandmother knew the crater
A Zeppelin left in Calverly Park
My father knew the clearing-up
Of a church, a hospital, a store

And he was one of the many
Whose schooling included the emerald glow
Of cathode-tube and blind flying
Somewhere unchallenged along the Channel

Here, the warning calls of fledglings
Tune their echoes of an erratic harmonic
Into the music of larksong, goldfinch, sparrow
That rinses the oaks and fine silver birches

The tree-boles here were neatly severed
Where the few fell in the hurricane:
And the bluebells sprang like wildfire
In advance of the regeneration

The open sky, blue, with a white trail fading
Keeps the dove ascending, and the acres of grass
Are crisscrossed with paths to the rose-garden yonder:
Deployments of heaven, pure strokes of colour

And the clean limbs of bathers sport in the sun
Two young men play tennis; the ricochet echoes
While children play scrambling herbaceous borders
Lingering secretaries link arms after lunch

All these years on, the joy of the park
Is the harmonic language of fathers and sons
The birches are silver, the bluebells abundant
And the talk on the lawns is familiar, urbane.

His memorial is unmemorable:
Deep in surroundings of flowering shrubs
Is a vision determined by holding of arms
Beyond gentle mounds of summer grass

Dowding

Cricket Week

1. Aubade

A bustling among the rhododendrons
The final putter of the heavy roller
Anticipation hovering like a hawk

Fourteen paces and a scrape of boot
A fresh guard facing, a practise swing
Sprung turf quivering under play

2. Le Midi

Morning startles with its green fizz
Edginess; nothing off the middle
Some alteration in the field

Defence, appeal; a risk, a throw;
Better brave shot than pad to dismissal
A hotblooded drive against the break

The crack of battle, running, cheers
Updates to scorecard, sudden news
Overwhelming skill or chance

3. Nocturne

Only the fluttering of a bat
Against the roundness of full moon
Only the purple quiet rising

All quiet, except the gentle flap of tents
Unguarded now, an empty camp
This gentle summer's evening

At An Exhibition: Trinity Arts

What was it you came to see?
Was it a recommended view
Or a tour which promised mystery?

Is this the outlook of your choice
Or a tick on some itinerary?
Does this piece here reflect your face

Or does it rather move your heart:
To travel to another place?
It all depends from where you start

And where you go in passing through:
Appreciation of this art
Demands a journey, asks of you

What was it you came to see?

Unnecessary Bits

Recently I've begun to notice
Odd little passageways, individual quirks
You hardly would think of in everyday passing
All sorts of strictly unnecessary bits
Larking around in respectable streets

Take the pattern of ironwork under this porch
Useful support for a functional awning
Neat holes would easily have lightened the casting
But instead there's a blowsy flower and some trailing
Rambling ivy looped over the space
In symmetrical crafting of arbitrary growth
Doing the opposite of what nature intended:
Gilding the lily, or casting nasturtiums?
Earning forever our new approval.

Where, or what at, would you draw the limit?
Elves in a conference, reptiles with teeth,
Lions to welcome the whistling milkman
Likeable squirrels of pensionable bent
Seem somehow essential, in a natural way

The Lovesong of J. Alfred Outcrop

welcome to fresh ground
whatever's on your mind
you can't buy cheaper than a
friendly atmosphere all welcome
beneath it is the cold bath built in 1702
due to restructuring of business
book now for christmas
quality and service
enquire at reception downstairs
many actors later famous played here
while keeping the existing 18th century facades intact
a tradition we maintain by selection of the finest
whatever a man sows that he shall reap
and so to bed
help us to help you
fill your rooms with rainbows
sans peur et sans reproche
easy access to advanced features
you could be sitting on a small fortune
reduced by £1 every day until sold
a suit counts as two items
there's something new in town
that feels as good as it looks
push button and wait for signal opposite
presence is protection

Antique Shop

If it's brass you're after,
Reflections to enrich your fire,
Tongs and scuttles, coppered pans
Something cheerful for your hearth,
Then look inside.
You may find fine
Filigrees or china,
Sketches, etchings,
Bung-stoppered jars,
Shelves of memoirs,
Distinguished glass,
Samplers, stamps,
Reflective walnut
Dressing-suites.
You may decide
That after all
You don't need brass
But a rather pleasant standard lamp.

Spring Fever

Hazel dangles like a Capri spoiler
Daffodils are upwardly mobile
Crocusses jive to their personal juice

I'll be glad when I've shaken off this cough
It's a new strain, I read in the Telegraph
The consequence of too warm a winter

The elders must know something
Spraying out blossoms this early in Feb
The market must be rising

Fractured cloud, and the wind's swung north-east
All the mothers are loaded with teat-swinging tots
Huddling easy, as warm as the earth, where

Crocusses jive to their personal juice
Daffodils are upwardly mobile
Hazel dangles like a Capri spoiler

Claremont Road

When you came bounding in and changed
From your spotless Sunday best pearl-grey
Into the rugby shirt that hugged your breasts
And the jeans which magnified each sway
And asked what I'd done, I ignored
Thoughts of Clydebank, looked away

From a peerless ballad of a wind of change
To magnolias bursting in the Easter blue
White, luxurious, patterned, lush
By laurels, timelessness of yew
I felt the bliss of happiness:
A private park soon changed my view.

Rusthall Rock

i find
most people
approach me from
the customary path and
talk as if i had no feelings
they point their fingers at my hunch
where i rock forward on my haunches
and make assumptions as to character
looking at me as if i'm some kind of a toad
which is a pity from my point of view
when they look from the other side
i'm more a dead ringer
for rodin's thinker
or a bust of cleopatra
anyway i'm in no position
to do much about it

Rusthall Rock

A Hint Of Sepia

Photography makes perfect art:
Take this: an honest horse and cart
Stood calmly by a water-trough
With an ostler trying not to cough

Behind his back, a pair of reins
To keep both profiles to the lens
A hint of sepia by the poses
Suggests a detail for the roses

In focus but soon made a bloom
By an artist in the drawing-room
To make this rural scene more couth:
A bit more positive than truth

It's no deceit: the hunt for pride
Insists we sweep all that aside
And concentrate on what first drew
Our interest when passing through

It's this that makes the Wells go round:
Beau Nash strolling through the town
A double-take which overlaps
Other, unembroidered, snaps

He shows a readiness to please:
Beneath that hat, a host at ease
Bequeathing, with a hint of tease,
Perfect smiling memories.

Beau Windows

I'm part of an ancient tradition
A serf with a spring in my heart
Chalybeate waters make good sons and daughters
By my troth, let sad humours depart

Fourth coach party from Scunthorpe
And they've cleared all the sponge-cake from Binns
Here's a couple or three completing their tea:
Good-day to you all, for your sins

I can't understand what they're saying
From a surfeit of false teeth and crumbs
If only they'd speak up, twixt tongue, lip and tea-cup
I'faith, how such languor benumbs

They've put on their bifocal Ray-Bans
They've picked up their waterproof togs
Wouldst thou fain now, prithee, take the water with me?
'Twill cure dropsy and mopsy and dogs

Still, at least they've got into the spirit
From the Vintry, or Duke, I'd assess
Ha Ha, my friends, merry: sing to sack, mead and sherry
Here's health to us all and Queen Bess

There's a matron from deepest Llandudno
Writing postcards on every bench
In the shadow of gold limes it's just like the old times
How farest thou, good seemly wench?

I'm part of that ancient tradition
Of slowing down ages diurnal
Come gather round, trippers, and let us be dippers
In that spring where hope is eternal

And Stay Out/Talkin' Tunbridge Wells

This must be Paradise: New Orleans jazz
Brassing the stomp in the Calverly Hotel
Full house folk-rock in the Assembly Hall
Iain blowing the blues downtown

Woke up this mornin', i got the blue-chip blues
Reelin' an' rockin', i surely paid ma dues
Debenture adventure left me nothin' but shoes

Goodtime shawling through dark streets
Sweet little schoolgirl and a dirty old Strat
Whisky in the jar, if you know where
Jimmy Walker, you've got a friend

Standin' here wonderin' will a Range Rover hol' my clothes
Necessary accessories, DJ 'n country-house brogues
Honey, Ceefax the Met man, see which way the wind blows

Somewhere in town there's a bit of baroque
Tippett and run in the Methodist Church
Schwarzkopf or Squeeze, we've all got the T-shirts
Dvorak whipping the old blue genes

Well i ride a late train, KV 3-1-4, Orpington
Lost th' woodwind, momma, as we were gettin' on
Only an oboe but one more is gone

This freeway to heaven, it's never-ending
12 of Purcell and four to the bar
A band of angels, or maybe the saints
A-pluckin' an' a-suckin' celestial harps

How To Get There

How to get where? It's the other side
Yes. I wouldn't go from here.
I'll do my best.

Straight ahead down Grosvenor Bridge
Past the Black Horse and Bob's DIY
Until you come to the traffic lights and then

Straight across up Camden Road
Past EM Models and Delicious 2
Until you come to the traffic lights and then

Left turn into Calverly Road
Past Caesar's grill and Bottoms Up
Until you come to the roundabout and then

Fourth right into Crescent Road
Past the wedding shop and pine boutique
Until you come to the keep left sign and then

Turn right beside the second one
The one before the Assembly Hall
Until you come to the lay-by there and then

Park roughly on the double yellow lines
Right in front of the County Court
Until you come to block the way and then

Hoot your horn until you hear
Excuse me sir, would you mind moving on
Then you ask a policeman.

I'm Not A Burglar, I'm A Poet

I'm stood outside an 'ansome 'ouse
I'm jottin' dahn ideas
When all at once a door's flung back
And this bloomin' lass appears

"I've seen you from inside," she's said,
"Up to no good, I know it:
"You've come to burgle us, no doubt,"
I've said, no, I'm yer poet.

I'm clockin' all vese gardings, see,
Vere's one what's 'edged in spikes
An' one wiv cabbigies in rows
An' one what's full o' bikes

"So what," she's said, with much disdain
"What's that to do with you?"
I fought to make a contrast, like,
Was somefink I could do

"So you could make us all a stock
"For folk to laugh about?
"There'll be no more of this," she's said,
"I'll fetch the silver out"

She's gawn indoors an' come back quick
Wiv silver gleamin' brightly
Nah need fer all o' dis, I've said
She's said "We've got off lightly"

I recommend this trick for free:
Whip out your ode and show it
All except up Camden Park:
Rottweilers don't like poets.

Lament On The Southern Region

Where are the Schools of mighty esteem,
Where are the classes we used to know?
The summer expresses of superheat steam
My Tonbridge and Sevenoaks long ago

Where's the bark of exhaust on High Wealden ridges,
Where are the classes we used to know?
Where's the hoot of the whistle through tunnels and bridges
My Tonbridge and Sevenoaks long ago

All that skill on the banks sent into retirement,
Where are the classes we used to know?
The old Schools were fine if you weren't a fireman
My Tonbridge and Sevenoaks long ago

They came in the fifties, those slab-sided carriages,
Where are the classes we used to know?
Rusting and rocking like loose-coupled marriages
My Tonbridge and Sevenoaks long ago

They may have been quicker, but had they the glitter
Where are the classes we used to know?
Demanding of little but fuel oil and fitter
My Tonbridge and Sevenoaks long ago

There's more to a train than a motorman leading
Where are the classes we used to know?
There's the power of passion, the whiff of good breeding
My Tonbridge and Sevenoaks long ago

Canon Hoare's Memorial

Much-loved, commemorated still
The scrupulous Canon of Canterbury
Turns east his forthright countenance
White as the clouds above the hill

His tower has the Gothic thrust
Buttressed firmly, heavy-blocked
Sandstone ecclesiastical
Four Apostles, mosses. Must.

The widening of St. John's Road
Moved him to accommodate
Processive traffic and its staff
Its ritual crossing, its high load

His Trinity's become a stage
His outlook now a bus garage
Telephone exchange and bank
A Trinity to fit the age

On the highest rooftop of the hill
A silver aerial of slats
Three-sided, symbol of the new
Spreads its voice invisible

To those of us who now receive
Transmissions of the upper air
Through mobiles, radios, TVs:
Sacraments we now believe

We who get our news from Sky
Not benevolent pulpits, shall
We find, too, the urge to raise
A canon here, to sanctify?

Canon Hoare's Memorial

Wellington Rocks

Bursting through turf
Like knuckles through leather

Prehistory thumped in a huddle of muscle
Unhinged, deeply fissured, no visible features

Sprawling reptilian, awaiting the heat
Collapsed in exhaustion

Canyons of the clenched fist:
Solid bluff, patina of sand

To the south, a lake of ice
Where dune-grass clings

Cumberland Walk: Autumn

Delightful walking: where's the guide?

We love such gardens, you and I
Glimpses of lawn, attractions of the other side

Through tunnels of swung boughs we stroll
Glancing left and right, our pleasant rôle

To view the best and not to pick up leaves:
Attendance to such lawns as these

Is for jobbing gardeners in boots.
We settle for glimpses of green shoots,

A stroll of joy: no obligation
Though hardly a tactic for a nation

Let's make our way back to the station.

Nomination

Soft ambience of Tiffany
"A brandy with your panatella?"
Not business, more exchange of view
Set in rooms of white and gold

Patterning the entrances of Calverly Road
Expectations of goodwill dance
Urgent among the Chrismas lights
Rings to look at, presents to find.

"Even though we're talking in millions
There's a market there if we price it right"

Standing in a doorway in Calverly Road
Amid arbitary pigeons, he compares
Notes and coinage, crumbs and paper,
Sings *have you heard* to a blue guitar

"Risky business, but we went ahead
Even when the foreign markets crashed, the States
Pushed us out there on the ledge
Right up with the pigeons, but we hung on in
Over all that song and dance and won the suit
Completely wiped the floor with them, got out, now
Here's to your good health and ours. I really would
Encourage you to stake your name"

In The Tea Shop

Some times I wonder why I collect
Art Deco, all the 30's set
Nordic champions, unerect
Stylised race of ideal jet

Personally I prefer Nouveau
Ecstatic fronds of intricacy
Under and over, winding to and fro
Rather stylish: more my cup of tea

Elegance, simplicity
The handsome curve, the perfect touch

So often you can barely see
All that detail, yet it's there, you know,
Neatly masking intimacy:
Shall we have biscuits now, or go?

Resolutions are so hopeless; no,
Ever since, I've not felt like much.
Perhaps I'll keep that lamp at least,
Recatalogue those matching sets
Or auction them. I must decide.
Collecting, keeping every piece,
Has cluttered up my attic: let's
Eliminate. I'll keep my pride.

An Evening Home

An Evening Home

In spring the cherry blossom will appear
There is a bench beneath the scented pine
You really could do worse than settle here

The thrushes chortle in the old-man's-beard
Where laurels merge into the box, a sign
In spring the cherry blossom will appear

My latest darling was a brigadier
So keen, so quick, his heart gave way to mine
You really could do worse than settle here

Each morning brings a change of atmosphere
Convolvulus attends on columbine
In spring the cherry blossom will appear

A game of whist? You mind your pennies, dear
While I've a single chance I won't resign
You really could do worse than settle here

A deal more perfect, simpler every year
Some cards go missing, but those left combine
In spring the cherry blossom will appear
You really could do worse than settle here

Coming From Nowhere

It all seems to be coming from nowhere
Rebounding like sunlight from terraced windows
Between the basking walls of Tunnel Road
Mattbikes and T.Sumner's Catering Hire

A chirruping, throstling Parliament
You can hear it fifty yards away
An invisible cacophony, questioning
Coaltits, finches, starling? Impossible,

Too small and hid, to tell. Two fling
Over the gardens of the neighbourhood
Straight to the heart of a single cupressus
Vanish and berth in the shaggiest green

Chattering stops. Silence
Surprises. Then one upward chirp
And the whole boiling beakshot's back,
Chattering hymnal, meeting communial,

Why not light, open gardens?
Next door has shrubs and an apple tree
The rooftops are airy, inviting:
Why choose a dark haven for chanting your song?

The air is no place for gathering views:
Flight's a defence, but best to survive
Is to flock with the swooping, or suddenly scut
Hedgerow to hedgerow, through the violence of light

Coming to earth in a tangle of branches
For throstling sessions in the tall cupressus
Where terraces echo uncomplaining
Sunlight, song, accelerating Cavaliers

Somebody comes out from behind a door
Shaking a rug to see what I'm doing.
They won't leave while they're watched
So I walk away, over the tunnel,

Scut down through Hill Street. If the Lord will
The Word of God will be preached here
On Lord's Day. 4.30. You are welcome
Wherever you are coming from.

Returning

It's not far away, I'm sure that we'll find it:
This country we're looking for, beautiful dream
Of deep lanes and oasthouses, garlands of hop,
Plentiful orchards and murmuring streams

It's nearer than ever, the signpost is certain:
This rambling footpath, thank goodness it's clear:
This cornfield was landscape, I can't quite remember,
There once was sweet chestnut; but it's beechwood I fear

It's close as a gate, there's no-one can close it:
This opening we're facing, where hedges and streams
Reach into deepness through garlands of hope,
Beautiful silence, invisible dreams.

Southern Hills

It's true what they say about Southern hills:
An easy stroll from foot to crest
Surrounded by clovers and the drowsy hum of bees

Against the Pennines, they're scarcely worth mentioning
If you like your hills ten miles off, melancholy, isolate
And your weather bleakly predictable

These hills are neighbourly, custodians of local news
Big news you can't see coming, no time for a coat
The beauty is, it's quickly over

You've sheltered, and so found yourself well dressed
For the sun which beams on intimacy:
It's true what they say about Southern hills.

A Bowl Of Cherries

The juiciest lessons were crammed in the orchard
Under the boughs in the sweet, level grass.
I can taste them all now, in a bowl of fresh cherries

Land-Rover diesel, the bump of a bomb-trailer
Haulage and swing of a five-bar gate
The blatance of sheep, irregular, honest.

Those cherries were favourite for their abandon
Great lofty thunderclouds galleoned in green
Towered eruptions, spectacular trunks

Oozing wild resin that stuck to both hands
And limed us like finches; the sprayer whined rainbows
Arching its mixture through dry-dripping alleys

Coppering our fingers in the weeks before picking;
Those strong sweeping branches, shifting, determined
Supported long ladders on swingers of trust

Gaining new height in the warm Kentish air
We'd a giddy look down through the dappling leaves
And a mouthload of gorgeousness deep in the tree

Plump Early Rivers, lush purple gushings
The flush of red on an Amber Heart
Or sour Morello, the one for keeping

We carved the stones and knew the taste
Of dodging through branches unencumbered
In those orchards of our learning

High Summer

A photograph in the garden
neatly captures a moment of joy
nearby the tumbling fuchsia
emeralds in the heart of your smile

Beautiful, lazy surprise
of highlights stranding the blond
while the hum of summer surrounds
each flowerhead sweet:
neat as a frond, delicious

Delight held in a picture-frame,
A moment of sheer happiness
Verifies the love we share;
In two dimensions under glass
Evoked, neat spirit
Spilling, gushing through the air

County Show

Show me the Garden of England
The hops and the apples and pears
There's views plenteous from an M & D bus
On a Wildrover ticket, upstairs

Show me the hop-poles at Beltring
With amber flowers crowning the bine
There's plenty of vendors, but a lack of Eastenders
While the oasts are remarkably fine:

Show me the Garden of England
The cattle, the goats and the ewes
The show doesn't stop when you're up on top
On a Wildrover pass, you can't lose

Show me the orchards of Malling
The riots of blossom and bees
The groaning great boxes of succulent Coxes
And luscious pears loading the trees

Show me the Garden of England
The cabbages, broad beans and peas
There's viewing select when you're double-decked
On a Wildrover just as you please

Show me the goosegogs of Farleigh
The strawberry cloches to boot
The blissful occurrence of black and red-currants
Wherever you look, there's more fruit

So show me the Garden of England
The hops and the apples and pears
There's views plenteous from an M & D bus
On a Wildrover ticket, upstairs

County Show

White Walls

To a child, the white walls and valleys
Are the biblical cities, shining
And the same white moon rises
As lit Bethlehem

Though the white walls are rendered in plaster
Though the pine trees are dusted with frost
Who would deny such happy conjunction
Who refuse such proof of rebirth

Home Is Where The Hills Are

Breathless on Mount Ephraim, a fine place for a hospital
With a view of homely hills and the Opera House
Towers of all the Saints below, the weathervanes of Trinity
Following the gusts of a fresh congregation

I wish I knew more about cumulus, you and I
Gathering air that billows from the sea
Across the High Weald: on the horizon
Something's gleaming on Strawberry Hill, bright and distant

Who was it said something about hills, I can't remember,
Quarries, rocks and hills, all distantly familiar:
Smothered with wild bracken and miscellaneous scrub,
Hills should be what they seem.

That path from the Pantiles at the edge of the Common
It catches me out, not that it's steep
Or I can't see the end of it, just that I'm finding
My legs aren't quite what they were. You know.

There's a lot to be said for being younger, I suppose
Wishing yourself among the walks and bursting rhodedendrons
Smothered in all that pollen, smothered in ecstasy
At least on the Mount, I know why I'm breathless

But the outlook *is* beautiful, almost as purple
As the writers would have it, and I like it up here
Where reminders of rock have houses built on them;
I'm glad our home is on these hills

Tunbridge Ware

You'll remember Tunbridge Wells:
Leafy highness of the Weald
Stained-glass windows, cricket, choirs
Elegant avenues' appeal
The mastery of airy spires:
Your souvenirs of Tunbridge Wells

Weave the time in Tunbridge Wells:
Where grace consorts on balconies
Parades of bayed Edwardians
Keep bright the blades of artisans:
Propriety, old euphony
The long chord held in Tunbridge Wells

A fresh heart's beating: Tunbridge Wells
A Place for buyers, passing through,
The Pantiles less the derring-do;
Near gentle Grove's cool retinue
King Charles the Martyr claims the true
Royal, loyal, Tunbridge Wells.

It's in the grain of Tunbridge Wells:
This shimmering, this bagatelle
Of tourers, rakes and mademoiselles
Of journeys, meetings and farewells;
The fuchsia shakes its soundless bell.
We'll meet again in Tunbridge Wells.

Also available from Heartland Publishing

Jon Horne
LYING ABOUT AMERICA

In the summer of 1992, Jon Horne, a young(ish) musician from Birmingham, decided to quit his job in a plastics factory and, like so many others before him, go off to Look For America. Unlike most of his predecessors, though, he found it.

Or at least the part of it that rode across deserts in big green buses singing *Psychokiller*, swam across muddy rivers to Mexico, and formed strangely moving relationships with rocks.

Lying About America is the story of a three-month trip from Boston to San Francisco and back amidst the most bizarre, funny, naïve, irritating, and in the end life-enhancing, group of people you'll ever encounter.

Some of it may be true. All of it is real.

ISBN 0 9525187 0 8
UK Price £6.95

for further information, please write to:

Heartland Publishing
55 Cherryfields
Sittingbourne
Kent ME10 1YW